Financial

Worries?

Try This!

… a member of the Launchpad Series

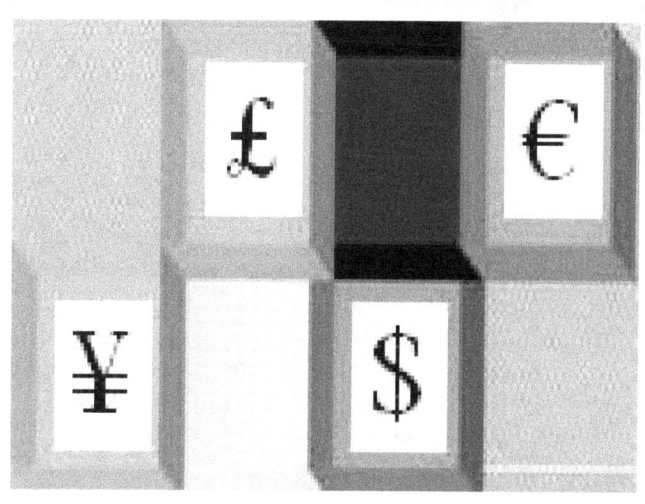

Copyright Information

Financial Worries? Try This!
© Royal Seeds International, February 2015
http://royalseedsinternational.blogspot.com/

Comments and order details should be directed to:
victorious_gem@yahoo.com

© *Royal Seeds International*

Table of Content

Preface

This book is a member of my **Launchpad Series,** designed to assist you in building a strong financial future through tested principles and uncommon practices of many years of personal development effort. It explains the fundamental steps to overcoming financial worries. Sometimes it seems as if everything happens all at once. Financial worries seem to pile up one on top of the other. If your business isn't going on as planned or envisioned, what is holding you back? You might probably say it is lack of capital, lack of employee, lack of time, so many family responsibilities and so on. But these reasons are not what caused your lack of financial success. These reasons are merely the results of a great cause – inability to respond to opportunities in time. Opportunities come as a flash and varnishes in no time. When dedication, hard work and constant devotion is mixed with opportunities, financial success is guaranteed.

Major thing in keeping a buoyant financial life is to be answerable to every of your financial actions. The truth is that accountability always helps to break bad habits and accumulate new ones. The biggest problem for many people is random or impulse spending. Impulse spending on eating out, shopping and online purchases is a big drain on your finances; it is the biggest budget breaker for many, and a sure way to be in dire financial worry. If you think you cannot hold yourself accountable; then secure the help of financial advisor.

In conclusion, your level of financial success is completely your decision. Change your thought pattern and align yourself to the course of positive actions and opportunities that comes your way; and you will be surprise at the rapid transformation the effect of the change will bring to you. Hence you can think your way to billionaire status or just acquire enough money to pay your bills. In either case, it is your desires, beliefs, thoughts and actions that get you over and constantly above financial worries of life.

Your season of financial empowerment is here!

Victor Peters – PhD

Financial Worries – What you must know

1

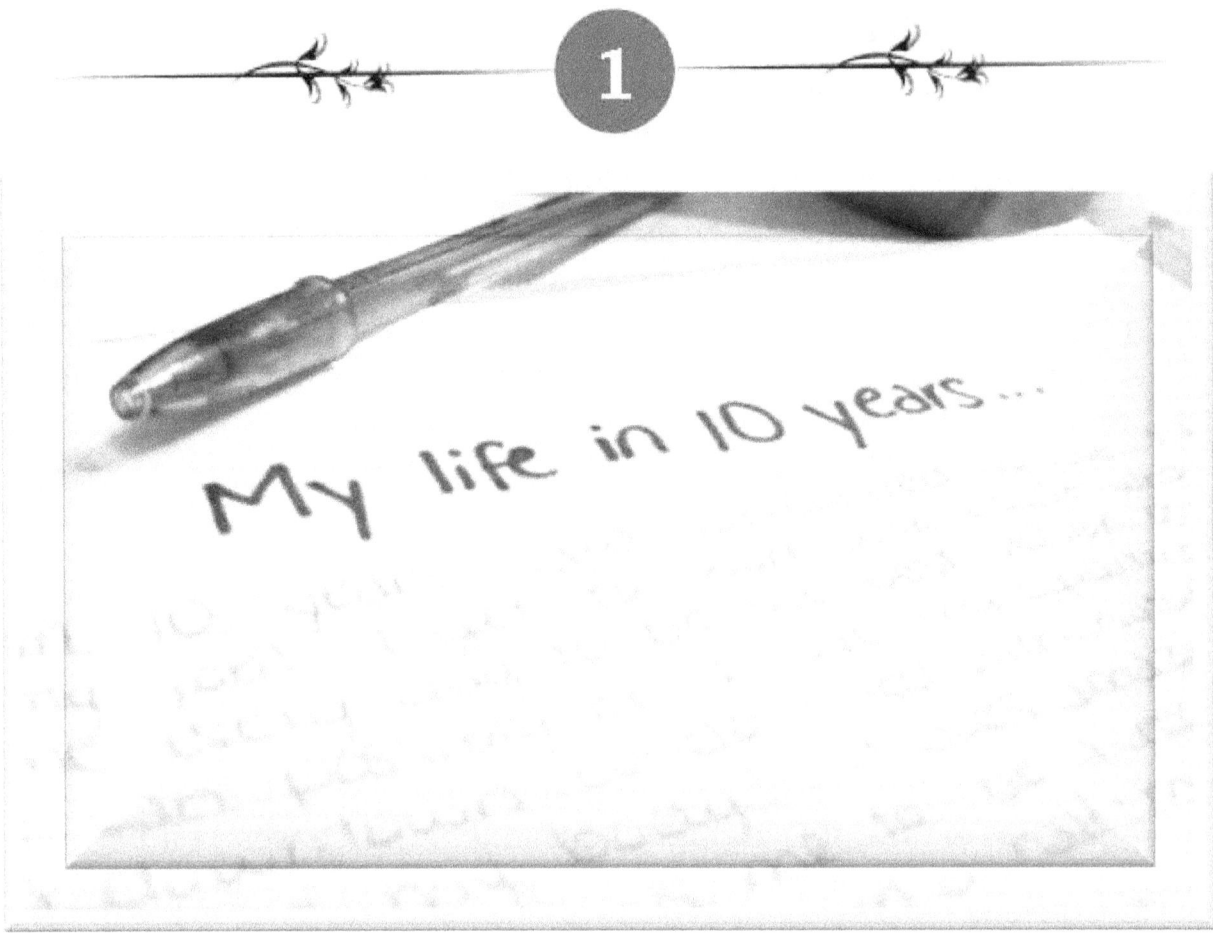

Worry by a layman's understanding is a state of insecurity that an individual passes through; it may be in the area of health, career, finance or family. When it has to do with money, it is being unsure where the next source of fund to handle your responsibility is to come from. Financial uncertainties or worries occur in everyone's life. However, the degrees of worry everyone experience depend on your societal status or class. Financial need of a restaurant attendant may not be more than a few hundreds of dollar for his feeding and one or two clothes to wear. A businessman whose business is not doing well definitely will require a higher level of financial fulfillment to end his worries. Whatever your class, financial worries affects every living being and therefore requires deliberate action on your part to overcome it. Just like gold and diamond are obtained by methodical exploration and hunting; so will a man find every truth connected with his financial worries and quality of life he lives if he is willing to dig deep into the mine of his soul. This means that he is the maker of his character, the molder of his life, and the builder of his destiny. He may choose to watch his life slip away in abject poverty, or control it; grab opportunities that come his way and therefore change the course of events to his advantage and survival through molding a new destiny for himself.

That you currently experience worries in your finance today does not mean that you cannot live in financial affluence and abundance tomorrow. However, most people results to fate, rather than taking deliberate steps to overcome this major concern of life. The societal class you find yourself today determines your level of influence on the people around you. To wield more influence, you need to be financially buoyant. If you take deliberate steps and positive actions on the issues raised in this book, you will elevate your societal status, improve your financial wellbeing.

Financial Insecurity Not Meant to Last a Lifetime

Financial insecurity is a state of been without or not having enough money. According to a popular author, tough time do not last, but tough people do. The truth of this statement depends on your resolve to conquer lack in your life. Financial insufficiency should not last your lifetime. But how long it persists depend on you. Are you willing to improve yourself? Positive improvement practices are essential to overcome financial lack. Poverty is a monster, and represents a huge figure that must be conquered in order to achieve financial buoyancy in our journey through life. Research has shown that those who plan for the future end up with more wealth than those who do not. Successful people are goal oriented: they set goals and develop a plan to achieve them. Be positive about life, and more importantly your future. You present circumstance is not a determinant of your tomorrow. But what you do with the opportunities that come your way today, determines what happens to you tomorrow. Change the way you think; have the achiever mentality. Don't confess success and always think poverty. The thought you allow in your mind is what germinates into character you exhibit; and the character you continually exhibit becomes your lifestyle.

Tricks of Negative Power behind Lack

There is a negative influence behind lack that control your mind to belief that being poor can be traced back to your ancestors (whether your immediate or past generation) or the privilege you don't have. It may also come in the form of picture painting of your current financial state. How that you are a good for nothing individual who can never achieve any success in life. If you encourage this thought in your mind for more than necessary, it will take root and control your physical world. Instead of encouraging negative words and phrases in your mind, choose positive words and phrases to help you build the life you want. The vision that you glorify in your mind, the ideal that you enthrone in your heart, is what you will build your life by; and consequently you will become. I have seen a man whose past generations never had access to basic amenities of life – clothing, shelter and food; but rose to become the Group Managing Director (GMD) of conglomerates of companies. Just the same way, I have seen a man who won a lottery of two million British pounds; and yet result to begin for money to eat later in life.

There is a mentality you have of yourself that can make or mare you. You should conquer negative controlling powers first in your mind and set the creative visualization spirit to work. Creative visualization begins in the mental/feeling/emotional world, but its results are evident in the physical world. Hence, thought supply the aim, purpose and direction; and our desires add energy to it. If you consciously, choose the thoughts, phrases and words that you encourage in your mind, your life will start to change. You will begin creating new situations and circumstances. You can overcome negative thoughts and build new ones, develop new skills and abilities, and even change your circumstances and attain anything that you truly desire in life.

As mentioned in one of my books, *Financial Success Toolkit*, good thoughts and actions can never produce bad results; likewise, bad thoughts and actions can never produce good results. As human being, we only begin to discover ourselves when we cease to be careless about the issues concerning our life, rather commences the search for hidden justice which regulates our life. When the truth is found, and we adapts our mind to that regulating factor, we stop accusing others as the cause of our poor condition; instead build up for ourselves a strong and definite goals of life, kick against negative circumstances, and begin to use them as aids to rapid progress, and as means of discovering the hidden powers and possibilities that nature has brought our way.

Getting Started and Goal Setting

Getting Started

When you are about to run a race, your initial preparation and hard work is important if you must win that race. Bad preparation results in bad outing. Friends and colleagues I'll like to ask you one question: what do you really want in life? For sure, bad circumstances exist. But the best we can give to any bad circumstance of life is to ensure we overcome it. Financial incapacitation is what leads to financial worries, and financial worries build up to engaging the backdoor principle of achieving financial success. Practically, as human beings we all want to live in surplus; so we desires to have our needs and wants met. But what happens when you desire to have and it seems those things are not coming your way? Instead of exercising patience, many take the law into their own hands. That is why we have evil occurrence all over the place today. Negative thoughts get registered in the mind faster than positive ones. A man who snatched a car at gun point did not just find himself at the spot where he committed the evil act, but has the whole idea played out in his mind overtime before he carries it out. Not just played out in his mind alone, that action took a better portion of his mind for it to gain acceptance and validity. When bad thoughts enter your mind, do you water it down or you get it uprooted? Financial insecurity is the root of bad thoughts; these thoughts if not controlled lead to so many negative vices including financial worries. Financial worry is one of such bad circumstance of life that is prevalent in most part of the world, and so requires deliberate effort to overcome it. What then does it mean to fight bad circumstances? It means as human beings we continually revolt against the negativity of our lives that tends to limit our happiness and social equilibrium with others. As an individual I have taken deep thoughts about life, and I discovered that we are the architects of all that happens to us in our journey through life.

To keep yourself out of financial worries, you have to keep improving on your financial discipline always, as well as taking important positive steps towards financial success. Aggressive financial actions such as taking good advice from financial experts, taking calculated risks, debt avoidance, buying your daily items where it's cheaper, participates in opportunities that comes your way and self-discipline; are some of the avenues to retain money, and they will help you minimize financial worries. These approaches will be discussed in more detail later. The motor industries will give a good analogy on continuous improvement. For instance, a vehicle manufacture by Ford motor company in the 1960s was very valuable at that time because it is the best effort around then. The same vehicle if reproduced and rolled into the market today will receive much less patronage from buyers, if not none. Each year, motor manufacturers follow market trends and buyers desires to produce the next series. Human tastes are changing continuously, and so must the manufacturer respond to customers' taste in order to get for their products, good share of the market. In all human endeavors there are exertions, and the strength of the exertion is the measure of the result you should expect.

Know yourself and what you want in Life

Everything you want should be yours: the type of work you want; the relationships you need; the social, mental, and aesthetic stimulation that will make you happy and fulfilled; the money you require for the lifestyle that is appropriate for you; and any requirement that you may (or may not) have for achievement or service to others. If you don't aim for it all, you'll never get it all. To aim for it requires that you know yourself and what you want." ~ Richard Koch

Financial worries seem to be piling up one on top of the other if no adequate management principle is put in place to check its proliferation. First thing is to know yourself or your ability in terms of spending power. Live your size per time and trust God for more; never you live beyond your means. Control your eyes and make reasonable decision when the need arise. Many live their life in obscurity, trying to create an impression that is never noticed by the person who they are trying to impress; and therefore bring about temptation that is unnecessary upon them for just no reason. A life of false impression will never add anything beyond temporary satisfaction to you; rather it takes away your possession. There was a friend of mine when I was growing up in those days, he will always buy clothes beyond his financial capacity just to impress girls around him. With all the false impression, he comes to me lamenting how the girls he is trying to impress were breaking his heart on daily basis.

How do you overcome spending temptation? Setup a budget for yourself and never exceed your budget. Refuse to borrow; be a man of discretion. By definition, discretion is having good judgment on a particular issue and it is the ability to say NO when you need to. It will preserve you and keep you above financial worries at all times.

The key to overcoming financial worries is living within your means. Spend less than you make and save money for the future and you can achieve financial sovereignty. It is that simple. Even a little bit of savings will accumulate and grow into significant amount over the long term. It is the trend over the long term that makes a difference. It is called the magic of compounding interest. A quick way to overcome financial worries is to pay attention to your cash flow and create the habit of saving. Yes, it is simple but it may not be easy to spend less than you make.

Cash Balance @ hand = Money Coming In - Money Going Out

Basically you want to have a positive cash balance at hand and save this excess money for other important need that may require your attention.

Finally, know what you want in life and pursue it vigorously. I'll like to let you know that nothing drops on a platter of gold for anyone in life without putting an equivalent amount of exertion towards what is desired. Frank Lloyd once said "I know the price of success: it is dedication, hard work and unremitting devotion to the things you want to see happen".

Goal Setting and Tracking

Identifying and setting clear, achievable goals is a crucial part of anyone's financial growth plan. A financial success goal is the exact time-dependent schedule of what is to be achieved over a period of time. For instance, in the next five years I plan to take my business to a level of total asset amounting to US$10 million. Of course, the business may be currently at a total asset capacity of US$300,000. Making the goal precise helps you determine how much effort you need to put in to get your goal accomplished. And on a pre-determined time interval within the period of the goal-setting, an appraisal is done to check if progress is being recorded or not.

There are three types of goals: short-term, mid-term, and long-term. Short-term goals are to be met in one year or less; mid-term goal is scheduled for between one to five years and long-term goal is for five years or more. For instance, vacations, gifts, and electronics are typical short-term goals. A down payment for a house is a common mid-term goal. Long-term goals may include business growth and development, saving for retirement and a child's higher education.

Tracking your goals is essential. The Financial Goals Chart will help determine the timeline for your goals and the amount of money you'll need to regularly set aside in order to reach them. You may find the numbers daunting or even not realistic based on your current financial situation. You may be able to increase your income and/or decrease your expenses or have to consider adjusting your goals. Determining your priorities is essential too. If you share your finances with someone else, discuss and set priorities together. It is not uncommon for couples to work at cross-purposes financially without even knowing it.

Major Contributors to Business Success

Financial success hinges on engaging two contributing factors – the inner factor – the mind; and the outer attributes – dedication, hard work and unremitting devotion.

Engaging the Mind for Financial Success

Your mind is an inward contributor to your financial success. Moreover, it is the source of what you engage in the physical. Engaging your mind is taking the bull by the horns. The subconscious mind regards the words and thoughts that get lodged inside it as expressing and describing a real situation, and therefore, endeavors to align the words and thoughts with reality. It works diligently to make these words and thoughts a reality in the life of the person saying or thinking them. The mind is the seat of the subconscious and therefore represents the awareness you receive on any issue of life. Whatever is executed by any mortal man in the physical; good or bad, first exist in the mind. Thoughts emanate from the mind; if given enough consideration overtime it gains support for physical manifestation. These thoughts are like magnetic currents. If you keep thinking about some event or action, it becomes a part of your life. This holds true when thinking about things you want and about things that you don't want. As you think, so you become. Your predominant, habitual thoughts and feelings determine whether you will achieve success or not, and whether you will feel satisfied upon realization or not. This means that you have to be more aware of your thoughts and feelings. It is important to learn to be more positive, less critical, and less worried. Then, when success is achieved, you can enjoy the happiness of achievement. Thoughts, attitudes and habits can be changed. The change does not come overnight. Some inner work is necessary. Positive thoughts and feelings make you happier and more receptive to success, and a positive disposition bestows upon you the ability to enjoy success when it comes.

For example, there is a big difference between "I am trying to increase my sales every week" and "I increase my sales 15% every week". In the later, you have put yourself in the state of mind of doing and having; but the former implies you are only giving it a casual approach (trying to do). This means your state of mind is in trying not actually doing, so you don't have a confirmation of the results expected. Changing your thoughts pattern must be repetitive to be effective. It is not possible to change your thought once and expect it to always produce the results you want. Modifying habits can be a daunting task to several people. Fortunately, after many years of research, Napoleon Hill discovers a common point relating to this difficulty. And he said "To be a success at anything in this world, you need at least desire, belief and action".

It is important to nurture your mind well because out of it precedes the wisdom to achieve success for your business. Your level of business success is a function of the state of your mind. The success you achieve is completely your decision. You can think your way to billionaire status or think enough just to accumulate enough funds to pay your bills and little more to spend. You cannot live a positive life with a negative mind; your business success begins from your mind.

Engaging Physical Attributes for Business Success

Even though the physical attributes give your business outward expression, the mind is where it all originates. The physical attributes that ensure business success are dedication, hard work and constant devotion.

Even though the platform to pull you out of financial worries is set before you, achieving your dream is your personal input. In other word, your dedication, hard work and unremitting devotion to duty will determine if you can pull through. But I belief every step we take in life is either with our being conscious or unconscious of its final end. Men are anxious to improve their circumstances, but are unwilling to improve themselves, they therefore remain bound. If you and I do not shrink from self-crucifixion we can never fail to accomplish the goals of success we have set for ourselves. This means that a man who is determined to acquire wealth must be prepared to make great personal sacrifices before he can accomplish his desires; and how much more is he who would realize a strong and vibrant objective of life – FINANCIAL FREEDOM? Our creator will always provide us with the OPPORTUNITIES, but grabbing the opportunity that comes your way is your own decision.

A) DEDICATION

Another name for dedication is commitment. It is the lubricating oil that greases your effort to succeed. It is to be excited about what you are doing. You cannot adjust your life around something if you do not care for it; love is what drives your motivation and allow you to invest your time and effort around that thing you love. If that sense of personal commitment is not there then there is no motivation. Therefore, it is motivation that keeps one from quitting any challenge of life. If the motivation is there, you will sacrifice your time; so we could also say that dedication is time, a whole ton of time in fact. You don't just become dedicated to something without your time involved. You become dedicated to it because of the amount of time spend on it. One wouldn't be considered dedicated to something if they spent just an hour a day on it; time and dedication go hand in hand. Be responsible and loyal to the course of action you belief in. Your body and mind must be up to full potential to accomplish the things you want to do when you are dedicated. You are dedicated to your course of action in life if you find yourself showing the following attributes:

- Put all your heart into achieving success in your course of action.

- Undiluted passion to pursue your course of action to a logical conclusion.

- Never give up at any time in the pursuance of your course of action.

- Be responsible to its outcome every step of the way.

B) HARD WORK

Hard work is the platform on which you can achieve everything valuable in life. If work is applying your ability, then hard work is applying your ability with focus and intensity to the exclusion of other possibilities. Some define hard work as anything you do that challenges you. And why is challenge important here? Why not just do what's easiest? Most people will do what's easiest and avoid hard work; and that is precisely why you should do the opposite. The superficial opportunities of life will be attacked by multitudes of people seeking what's easy. The much tougher challenges will usually see a lot less competition and a lot more opportunity. There is an African gold mine two miles deep. It cost tens of millions of dollars to construct, but it's one of the most lucrative gold mines ever. These miners tackled a very challenging problem with a lot of hard work, but ultimately it's paying off.

Strong challenge is commonly connected with strong results. Sure you can get lucky every once in a while and find an easy path to success. But will you be able to maintain that success, or is it just a coincidental? Will you be able to repeat it? Once other people learn how you did it, you will find yourself overloaded with competition.

When you discipline yourself to do what is hard, you gain access to a realm of results that are denied everyone else. The willingness to do what is difficult is like having a key to a special private treasury room. The nice thing about hard work is that it is universal. It doesn't matter what industry you're in — hard work can be used to achieve positive long-term results notwithstanding the explicit.

I'm using this same hard work principle in building this personal development book. I put in a lot of valuable time possessions that are precious to me in getting things done; I put the writing of this book on top hierarchy on the scale of preference. I try to address topics that other people don't and bypass the low hanging fruit. I strive to explore topics deeply and search for the gold. I do lots of reading and research. I write lengthy articles and give my best ideas away for free, so I'm constantly forced to better my best. It's a lot of hard work. But I want this to be the kind of book that people will still be looking for ten years from now. Writing a book like this is at least ten times harder than the kinds of books I see dominating the psychology section of bookstores today. But most of those books will be off the shelves in a year, and few people will even remember them.

Definitely, hard work pays off. The greater your capacity for hard work, the more rewards fall within your grip. The deeper you can dig, the more treasure you can potentially find. Being healthy on its own is hard work. Finding and maintaining a successful relationship is hard work. Raising kids is hard work. Getting organized is hard work. Setting goals, making plans to achieve them, and staying on track is hard work. Even being happy is hard work (true happiness that comes from high self-esteem, not the fake kind that comes from denial and diversion).

Hard work goes hand-in-hand with acceptance. One of the things you must accept is that those areas of your life that won't succumb to anything less than hard work must be pursue with the mindset of acceptance. Perhaps you have had no luck finding a fulfilling relationship. Maybe the only way it's going to happen is if you accept you're going to have to do what you have been avoiding. It is time to accept that the path to your goal requires absolute discipline. Perhaps you want to increase your income. Maybe you should accept that the only way it will happen is with a lot of hard work. Your life will reach a whole new level when you stop avoiding and fearing hard work and simply surrender to it. Make it your ally instead of your enemy. It's a potent tool to have on your side. The following are signs that you currently embrace had work in your personal area of endeavor – be it in business or other goals of life:

- Survive the initial storm of starting a new business.
- You have reproduced yourself through your staff so as to expand your business.
- Establish a thriving business on dint of hard work.
- Bring in and teach your beneficiaries the rudiments of your business.

C) CONSTANT DEVOTION

Constant devotion to anything you belief in will propel you into achieving the success attached it. Action is the foundational key to all success in life. Your life does not get better by chance; it gets better by continuous change you applied to it. Every day do something that will inch you closer to a better tomorrow. By changing nothing, nothing changes. Problems remain the way they are because people are busy defending rather than finding solutions to them; so stop wasting time defending that problem and work on addressing it instead. In the real sense of it, the secret of life is not in what happens to you, but what you do with what happens to you. The truth is that we all have abilities; but the results we get from our abilities vary widely because it depends on how we use it. The best preparation for tomorrow is to do today's work extremely well. The secret of getting ahead is getting started and giving a constant devotion to your course of action. If you don't go after what you want, you'll never have it. If you don't ask, you don't receive, and by not asking the answer is synonymous to not having hat you want. If you don't step forward, you're always in the same place. The following attributes of personal constant devotion will help you achieve your goals:

- Nothing in the world can take the place of persistence.
- Have an addicted life-style to everything about what you belief in because it determines your future.
- If it is business, be a guru in it by studying every aspect of the business through continuous knowledge improvement – TRAINING/WORKSHOP attendance etc.
- Put in high degree of efforts commensurate with your future expectations always.
- Know that a journey of a thousand miles must begin with a single step; so ensure you are moving forward always.

- The world is not all sunshine and rainbows. It's a very mean and nasty place and I don't care how tough you are it will beat you to your knees and keep you there permanently if you let it.

Financial Improvement Practices

Overcoming financial worries rests predominantly on instituting financial improvement practices and setting up a budget for yourself; as well as sticking to your budget. It is important to continually monitor your spending, savings, and investments and adjust your plan as necessary. Tracking your expenses on an ongoing basis will help you to see when you should stop spending because you have reached your limit in a particular aspect of your budget. You can use accounting software or a computer spreadsheet to track your expenses. There are also some computer budget programs that automatically track and categorize your debit and credit card purchases. If you overspend one month, try not to get discouraged. No one is perfect. If it happens often, you may need to readjust your plan so that it is more practical. The following financial improvement practices will assist in establishing financial stability and reduce your financial concerns.

Be able to distinguish between your need and want

It's great to pursue our dreams and have the life we want. But try to put a demarcation between your need and want. Your need are what is necessary and compulsory you must buy while wants are those things you desire but not so essential. Best thing to do is to first take care of what you need, and then consider what you don't need but really want later if you have budget surplus.

Build an Emergency Fund

Keeping some money aside can help ensure that you are covered during times of financial worries. This could include job loss, illness, disasters, or some other calamity. These things do happen, we just don't know when and how they will take place. So be prepared.

Spend Less than you Make

This one should be common sense, though realistically everyone has different life situation. What might be simple and no-worry for some people might be incredibly challenging for others due to their current circumstances. Regardless, we should strive to increase the gap between income and expenses.

Pay off Credit Cards on Time

The idea of carrying credit card balances just seems so normal to many people. I think that unless it's absolutely unavoidable, and basic needs can't be met due to financial distress; please try to avoid carrying credit card balances.

Control your Emotions when Shopping

Some people just let emotions get the best part of them when shopping. Having self-discipline can be a great initiative not only for finances, but for other aspects of life as well. Good judgment can be a great antidote for excess emotion when shopping, and an essential part of financial success.

Conduct Appraisal on your Spending Periodically

From time to time do assessment of your spending. This might be on monthly basis or bi-monthly. It implies checking your last month expenses and matching it with your set budget for that month. If your expenses are more than what you earmark in the budget for that month, it means you overspent and you need to check it.

Accountability

Main thing in keeping a buoyant financial life is to be answerable to every of your financial actions. The truth is that accountability always helps to break bad habits and accumulate new ones. The biggest problem for many people is random or impulse spending. Impulse spending on eating out, shopping and online purchases is a big drain on your finances; it is the biggest budget breaker for many, and a sure way to be in dire financial tension. If you think you cannot hold yourself accountable; then secure the help of financial advisor. One of the most beneficial aspects of having a financial advisor is the fact that you are in some manner accountable to them. The simple human desire to appear competent to someone else is often enough reason to restrict your spending when you know you'll meet with your financial advisor to go over your portfolio. However, using the service of a financial advisor is not the only way to be accountable. A spouse or a friend can serve the same purpose.

Continuous Knowledge and Skill Development

Your skills, knowledge and experience are the biggest asset you have. The value of your future earnings will depend on them. Your job and future career is the most important factor in achieving financial independence and security. Improving on these three assets opens the door of opportunities to you. Invest in skills and knowledge acquisition from time to time. The skill and knowledge you have today if not improved upon will become outdated tomorrow. I made a strong decision sometime back on knowledge acquisition that brought a huge door of opportunities my way today.

Cultivate the Habit of Saving

Nothing beats having a bank account that you can turn to when life gets a bit hard. Making sure that you always have money stored away will definitely give you some peace of mind. Another way to do this is to have a time deposit account. Saving is easier if you make it an automatic process. If you have direct deposit through work, you should be able to have a portion of your paycheck deposited into your savings account. Additionally, many financial institutions allow you to set up a periodic automatic transfer of funds from your checking account to your savings account. Start by simply trying to follow your budget. Once you can do this then the next step is to be able to save money. Saving money requires you say no to yourself when you have the urge to spend it.

Become Financially Literate

Making money is one thing; saving it and making it grow is another. Financial management and investing are lifelong endeavors. Making sound financial and investment decisions is important in achieving your financial goals. The more knowledgeable and experienced you are in financial matters, the fewer mistakes you will make. Research has shown that people who are financially literate end up with more wealth than those who are not. There is a strong monetary incentive for becoming financially sophisticated. Taking the time and effort to become knowledgeable in the areas of personal finance and investment will pay off throughout your life.

Take Calculated Risks

Taking calculated risks can be a prudent decision in the long run. You might make mistakes along the way, but remember, mistakes are the lessons of wisdom. Also, when you are young, you can recover faster from financial mistakes, and you have many years to recover. You often learn more from your mistakes than from your successes. Taking calculated risks when you can afford to do so is necessary to get ahead financially. Playing it safe might be a bigger mistake in the long run.

Conduct Appraisal of your Set Goals Periodically

From time to time conduct occasional appraisal of set financial goals to see what have been achieved and what is remaining. This is a very clear way of knowing what you have been able to achieve and what to be improved upon.

Be a Planner

Research has shown that those who plan for the future end up with more wealth than those who do not. Successful people are goal oriented: they set goals and develop a plan to achieve them. For example, if you set a goal to pay off your student loans in two years, you'll have a better chance of achieving this goal than you would if you merely said you wanted to pay off your student loans, but failed to set a timetable. Become a planner. Set goals and develop an action plan to reach them. Even the process of writing down some goals will help you to achieve them. Being goal oriented and following a plan means taking control of your life. It is an important step toward improving your financial independence and security.

Live According to your Size

This one should be common sense anyway; you know what you earn, so let your income guide you on what kind of lifestyle you should live. For instance your salary dictates that your spending should be among the middle class; but rather you are copying a friend whose spending is among the top class. For sure, you will soon be in financial tight corner. What might be a simple, no-worry for many people might be incredibly challenging for others due to their current circumstances. So be guided by your spending lifestyle.

Eliminate and Avoid Debt

It is a popular saying that the borrower is a servant to the lender. Some individuals are so comfortable with debts that they keep borrowing at every opportunity. Most of these individuals are the ones that buy thing on impulse. They have no budget, and there are no investment plans for the future. Credit card is seen today as an evil tool of wealth destruction because of impulse buying. If you've got credit cards, personal loans, or other such debt, you need to start a debt elimination plan. List out your debts and arrange them in order from smallest balance at the top to the largest at the bottom. Then focus on the debt at the top, putting as much effort as you can into eliminating them. This could take several years, but it's a very rewarding process, and very necessary.

Take Advantage of Opportunities

Taking advantage of opportunities in life starts with simply saying yes to them when they come around you; opportunities are not always exclusive to an individual, rather they are open to many. Others might grab them if they stumble on it. If you hesitate, you may lose out. Decision–making is what delay taking advantage of opportunities. While taking your time to make decision on an issue, you should also be aware that your decision is time constrained. If longer than necessary, it may cost you a great deal of regret.

Great opportunities often come from your own enormous ideas, so seat down and think. If you're negative about yourself, you'll just limit possible options available to you. This is not a good state of mind to be in. Opportunities and risk-taking often go together. If you cannot take risk, it is certain that opportunities will always pass you by. Someone who is a great risk-taker is sure to succeed; if that success is not seen around him now, give it time it will come. There is no way you can cage a risk-takers success; it will always come to be. The best opportunity is often the riskiest. Someone starting up a new business is not only taking a risk, but also taking advantage of an opportunity. Door of opportunities are never closed, and is not limited to the business field alone. You can look for, create, and take advantage of opportunities within your profession. Keep in mind not all opportunities result in promotions. They may be new challenges or increased responsibilities. It may allow you to gain experience, or prove to others your various skills and abilities. Opportunities do not guarantee an immediate increase in pay, and may require more work in the short term. Too many times employees miss out on opportunities because it requires more work for the same pay. What they do not realize is that their manager is giving them an opportunity to learn a new skill or demonstrate the ability to perform a task, either of which would make them eligible candidate for promotion in the future.

While not all opportunities come with financial rewards attached, they may instead offer you the ability to learn, develop, and demonstrate new skills which may be required for future promotion. Unfortunately, employees sometime miss out on these opportunities because there was no immediate or instant gratification attached to it. Instead, they consider the extra workload as a detriment instead of an opportunity. Understandably, everyone wants to make more money, and wants to get paid for their effort; taking on extra responsibilities is an investment in your career. As someone possibly new to the corporate world, you should concentrate on building your resume for future job advancement. Most employers want individuals with experience for higher level positions. By assigning added responsibilities, supervisors are providing their employees with a way to obtain this experience while still maintaining their current position. Consider it to be on-the-job training for your future job. While excelling in new responsibilities such as preparing a report or creating a work schedule do not give any monetary rewards at present, you are gaining valuable experience which makes you more promotable in the future. When interviewing for a future job which lists "ability to create a work schedule" as a job requirement, you can confirm you not only have the ability, you also have the experience. You took the opportunity to proactively become more promotable instead of waiting for the promotion to come to you. My advice is that you take advantage of every opportunity you are given in an organization or that comes your way in the course of business. On the job activities, training classes, books, and the internet are all excellent ways to learn and grow. Demonstrating the initiative to learn new responsibilities will make you promotable, if not at your current job, then at another company. Also, take the time to make your own opportunities. Instead of waiting for opportunity to come knocking on your door, you could also drive over to opportunity's house instead. Once you have conquered your normal work duties, ask your supervisor for additional responsibilities.

Managers love employees who show initiative. Use these opportunities as a stepping stone for better things to come.

Specific Place where You can Find Immediate Help

Network marketing is one area of business that is making a lot of people rich nowadays, especially if you plan to build a residual income for your family over the years. In the past I have always been skeptical about this type of business because a few of them had refused to yield good results to me. However, a trusted friend of mine introduced me to Secure Future International (SFI) sometimes ago. Initially, I did not want to join, but when he presented his membership commission payment index to me I was shocked. This is a guy I know has unresolved financial issues all around him. All of a sudden you see him buy expensive things. His latest monthly earning as at the time of writing this book was US$ 1,872; and it keeps growing overtime. Apart from this he has a TripleClicks PAYONEER debit card from the same company where he receives his payment. With all these evidence, I knew it must be real so I decided to join. Just 10 months as a member, my commission payment index was US$248.48 as shown in the image below.

Your Current Account Balance: $ 248.48

Month/Year	Total Commissions	Prior Balance	Adjustments	Fee	Deduction	ACH	Accum	Actual Amt
1/2014	$2.87	$0.00	$0.00	$0.00	$0.00		N	$0.00
2/2014	$7.07	$2.87	$0.00	$0.00	$0.00		N	$0.00
3/2014	$12.38	$9.94	$0.00	$0.00	$0.00		N	$0.00
4/2014	$22.32	$12.38	$0.00	$0.00	$0.00		N	$0.00
5/2014	$30.38	$22.32	$0.00	$0.00	$0.00		N	$0.00
6/2014	$77.07	$30.39	$0.00	$0.00	$0.00		N	$0.00
7/2014	$120.48	$77.07	$0.00	$0.00	$0.00		N	$0.00
8/2014	$177.07	$120.48	$0.00	$0.00	$0.00		N	$0.00
9/2014	$248.48	$177.07	$0.00	$0.00	$0.00		N	$0.00

🛒 YOUR STORE

TripleClicks™

🔰 SAFE & SECURE

VERIFIED BY
GeoTrust
Carson Service...
CLICK 31.10.14 06:38 UTC

⚑ SUPPORT

Support/Help
24-hour Knowledge Base
Contact Your Sponsor/Upline
Contact Us

⇄ TRANSLATE

Select Language ▼

 💬 What others are saying about SFI
I was very lucky to find SFI. It helps me to generate more income even if I am just staying at home. With its great team leaders on my side and simple automation, you can build a successful

About Us

Privacy Policy

I once thought that events in life come by luck, but soon know that time and chance happens to them all. I don't think I want to keep away this secret from you because getting you on the pedestal of financial success so you can overcome financial worries is the main goal of writing this book. Use the FREE gateway below to register. Welcome to your season of positive progressive change for financial empowerment!

http://www.sfi4.com/14507379/FREE

What exactly is on the unique scorecard of this company?

- 16th successful year in the business (29th for SFI's parent company)
- 1.6 million affiliates

- 3 million TripleClicks members
- 94,000+ commissionable products
- 6,709 E-Commerce Affiliates (in 168 countries)
- 169 LocalPay Merchants (in 39 countries)
- 2,768 – TripleClicks.com's global popularity rank (source: Alexa.com)
- Millions – Monthly commissions paid out to affiliates (in US Dollars)
- Do you know that as from the second month, each month you re-qualify as an Executive Affiliate (EA2), you are given $220.00 worth of products for FREE?

Perhaps, you my guest reading this book today may have being thinking of securing your financial future. The current job is possibly not going to give you enough pension money at the close of your work life or retirement; or possibly you don't even have a job. Then you have a chance right in front you. The vision that you glorify in your mind, the ideal that you enthrone in your heart, is what you will build your life around; and consequently you will become!

Prepare for your tomorrow today with NO financial commitment, but completely FREE to start. Try it out. If it does not go the way you expect you can unsubscribe, no string attach. It works for me and that is why I am sharing it. Opportunities are short-lived. You need to be quick in order to get the most out of them. The business world of today is filled with turbulence. And according to experts, turbulence rather than tranquility is the normal expectation of most business owners. As a matter of fact when business brings profit continuously for the owner over a range of time, he is surprise. This is because in his mindset the business world is unstable and complicated, and positive results are not to be expected on a continuous basis. Call it a slow down or a recession, the impact is the same – times are challenging. Today's business world requires effectiveness with change, strong communication and full awareness of every detail of your business. You must live by a strategic plan, one that is clear, focused, accountable and empirical. You must rally your organization to be on the go for opportunities – review every aspect of your business, consider every situation, know trends, needs and challenges and respond with ways to add value.

In all human affairs there are efforts, and there are results, and the strength of the effort is the measure of the results. Gifts, power, intellectual capability, and spiritual possessions are the fruits of efforts; they are steps taken, thoughts completed, or vision realized. However, the thoughtless, the ignorant, and the indolent, seeing only the apparent effects of things and not the things themselves, talk of luck, fortune, and chance. Yes chance! It will always come to you at your own time. Seeing a man grow rich, they say "How lucky he is!" another will say "How highly favored he is!" One thing I have come to understand about life is that time and chance keep resurfacing themselves to mankind because nature will always work on our mind's thinking and belief.

Seek Further Investment Opportunities

When money begins to roll in, continuously seek for investment opportunities so you can strengthen your financial muscles and expand your financial base. Investment opportunities will help you to establish a strong financial foundation for your future. However, this must be with caution because not all investment is good. Observe the business climate of such opportunity before committing yourself. My resolve not to invest in stocks sometime back cleared me from the trouble that came when there was a total crash of the stock market sometime ago. An investment on landed properties for instance, is a good decision. Land appreciates continuously. The growth of your investments over time will be amazing if you start early. Do a little research, but whatever you do, start now!

Get Good Deals for All Your Purchases

Get good deals for all your purchases and put back some money into your treasury. Money accumulates in bits; remove one cent from a dollar and what you have left is ninety nine cents. When this entire cutback accumulates from various sources, you will be surprised of the amount you have saved. Some of the best financial advice ever given is to buy low. If you are able to hold your finance stable in the current economy you are positioned to avoid future financial hardship. The real estate instability has left many banks holding too many houses. It has also created a huge rental market. If you have some money to invest now is the time to buy rental housing.

Transfer buying is a strong strategy of SFI that allows you to buy your regular daily need items at TripleClicks.com by transferring your purchase to your store. This means you are earning commission on your own purchase and using your purchase to qualify for your monthly affiliate status. For instance, I use to buy Advanced Liquid Nutrition every two weeks from a store close to my house, but since joining SFI. I purchase this item from TripleClick.com as standing order. With each purchase is 1500 VersaPoints (VP) which is enough for my EA qualification for the month; buying two units' gives 3000VP which is more than qualify me naturally as an Executive Affiliate (EA) each month. Apart from this the regular price outside is $54.00; but from TripleClicks.com I buy at $35.80. This is a huge savings for me. My qualification as EA each month gives me access to numerous benefits. Some of these include:

a. Co-sponsored affiliates to strengthen my team and help me earn more cash rewards;

b. Up to 20 FREE T-credits (worth US$ 39.80) for my purchases online at TripleClicks.com;

c. US$ 10 Cash reward in my second month as TEAM LEADER;

d. US$50 cash reward I can WIN in daily draws for one full year for making E365 FINALIST;

e. Thousands of dollars in direct commission on sales made through my TripleClicks referral, SFI affiliates etc. It is UNLIMITED; my sales volume determines what I get.

Even if you are not an SFI affiliate member yet you can purchase most of your daily need items from TripleClicks.com using the gateway:

http://www.tripleclicks.com/14507379

Deal of the day is another opportunity to buy at reduced price at TripleClicks.com. Deal of the day items sometimes have up to 80% price slash from the regular price. This is wow offer and it takes place every day.

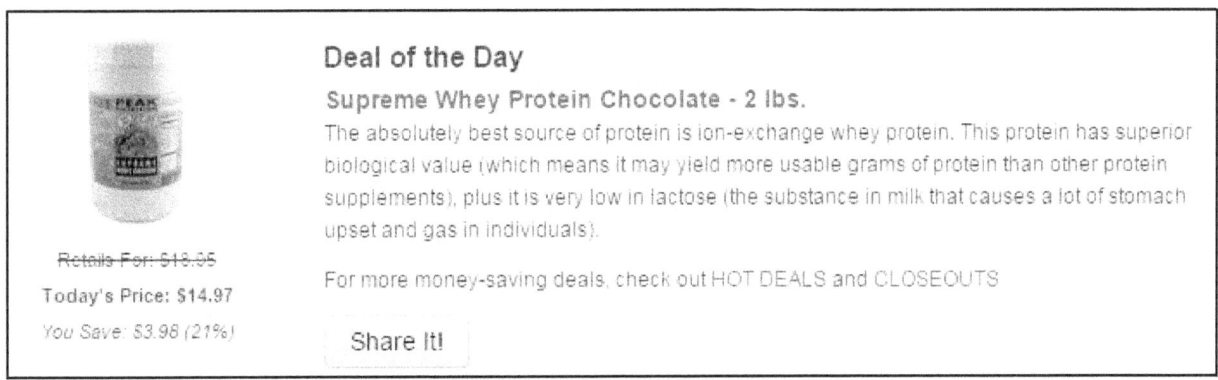

Self-Determination is Key

Overcoming financial worries in life requires extreme self-discipline, self-determination, strength of mind and positive personal actions. Self-discipline is self-control and self-determination is the willpower you apply toward achieving your goals in life. Both are inseparable from one another because without self-discipline, self-determination will not be in progress. Likewise, self-determination lacks meaning without self-discipline. Self-determination is the formidable force that helps you to hold on while pursuing a particular goal of life not minding the challenges that tends to keep you out of focus. It is the main instrument you use in conjunction with endurance, restraint and perseverance in the face of these challenges. One of the numerous life challenges people face is financial worries. I must say here that journey through life is like walking through entanglements, and your challenges are the entanglements. How quick you are able to remove this muddle determines how fast you can progress through life.

It is pretty clear that self-determination, an inner strength is the ability to proceed and carry out specific plans and actions despite internal resistance, external obstacles, and discomfort. For instance, when you have to meet someone you don't like you keep postponing the meeting; and therefore get worried constantly about it. You can equally choose to ignore the repulsiveness and do what you need to do without restrain. There are number of factors you should embrace in the pursuit of self-determination. Most of these factors engage your strength of mind and personal deliberate action in the direction of what you want to accomplish.

Conscious Effort

Conscious effort talks about the mindful steps you take toward actualizing a particular goal. The effort applied in moving a load from a location A to another B depend on the weight of the load and the distance through which the load must be moved (distance AB). If the load is just a ten kilogram bag of cement for instance; and is to be moved through a distance of five kilometers. The effort required can be calculated as follows:

$$\text{Effort applied} = \frac{Load}{Dis\tan ce} \rightarrow \frac{10}{5}$$

Effort applied = 2 units.

Just the same way, the effort required to push a car of 5000 kilogram through a distance of 1 kilometer is estimated to be 5000 effort unit. Definitely, the same effort cannot be applied to the two scenarios described above. The quality of the goal set can be compared to the amount of load while the duration to accomplish the goal is synonymous to distance.

Conscious effort implies deliberate application of energy towards meeting a set goal in life. To move the load away from its initial location, the effort applied must be greater than the weight of the load. In this case the weight of the load is the challenge you have to overcome in order to move your aspiration to its new location. Conscious effort is therefore the deliberate application of your willpower and strength of mind to overcome the challenges that comes your way in the actualization of your life goals. It is certain that every ambition in life has challenges attached to it. Your resolve to overcome these challenges is what gives you the breakthrough you desire.

Overcome Laziness

A lazy man will always find fault with everything he does, blame situation and circumstances for not being able to achieve goals set before him irrespective of how simple that goal can be. To overcome financial worries in life you cannot afford to be lazy.

There is a proverb that says '*a diligent man eats whatever he wants, but a lazy man eats whatever he can find*. The implication of this statement is that the diligent man can afford anything he wants to eat, but the lazy man has no choice than to eat whatever he finds. Laziness has rubbed many of their destinies in life because they choose not to embrace hard work. Hard work never kills, but laziness kills easily. When you can't afford what you want, then you have already being financially castrated. Financial castration has led many into committing suicide and others forced into going through the backdoors to gain financial success in order to overcome financial worries. The hand of the diligent bears the rule. Friends', being diligent at what you do is part of self-determination to succeed.

Persevere and Excise Patience

In your quest to overcome financial worries, when you put in conscious effort and conquer laziness; match these attributes with perseverance and patience. Many go through the backdoor to achieve financial success because they lack patience and perseverance. My observation of people who achieved financial success in the past is that they embrace patience and perseverance. An important parts of these two all important ingredients for financial success is living within your means. In order word, living within your means is part of perseverance and patience. Spend less than you make and save money for the future and you can achieve financial independence. It is that simple. Even a little bit of savings will accumulate and grow into significant savings over the long term. It is the trend over the long term that makes a difference. Don't live a life of shadow; rather let your lifestyle reflect your financial status or size at that moment. It is no wisdom when you know you cannot afford a two bedroom apartment, but just because you have a friend living in a three bedroom; you went and hire a three bedroom apartment to let your friend know that you are in the same class. Agreed, you have elevated your housing status to three bedroom; when it comes to making payment for the house after your rent expires will you call your friend to assist you in offsetting the rent? Wisdom is the stability of your times. Instead, persevere and be patient. It is a matter of time you will get there. So don't eat your tomorrow today. Be wise.

Never Accept Defeat and Never Give up

Most people are quickly overthrown by the force of defeat, and therefore give up. If you have a goal of what you have set to achieve, keep up with the vision. It is something obvious, that each passing day that do not produce positive energy towards achieving your goal can bring frustration your way; I will advice you don't give up. It is an exceptional thing in life to take a leap at success of any kind the first time and achieve it. Cars and airplanes are two important and very useful discoveries of our time today. If you get to know the number of times the inventors of these valuable assets had failed before these things come into existence, you will be overwhelmed. But rather than allow the force of defeat to overtake them, each failed attempt is seen as one of the many ways that things should not be done. So they retrieve their steps and start all over. Those failed attempts have added to your experience in that area of endeavor, and therefore teaches you not to go in that direction anymore. If you don't accept defeat, for sure you will not give up.

Drop off Negative Habits and Traits

Your thought crystallizes into habits, and habits solidify into circumstances. You can overcome negative habits and build new ones, develop new skills and abilities, and even change your circumstances and attain anything that you truly desire. All this does not happen overnight. It needs time, and depends on how sincere you are in your efforts, and on how much time and focus you put into changing your negative habits into positive ones. This is mental work, and you need to keep an open mind and be willing to take action when necessary.

Your predominant habitual thoughts type and feelings determine whether you will achieve financial success and overcome financial worries or not; and whether you will feel satisfied upon its realization or not. This means that you have to be more aware of your habits, especially the negative ones. It is important to learn to be more positive, less critical, and less worried. Then, when success is achieved, you can enjoy the happiness of achievement. Thoughts, attitudes and habits can be changed. The change does not come overnight. Some inner work is necessary. Positive thoughts and feelings make you happier and more receptive to success, and a positive disposition bestows upon you the ability to enjoy success when it comes.

Take it as a challenge, and pay more attention to your habits. Find out what kind of habits you are into and what kind of results you get in connection with them. If your habits are positive that's okay. However, if your habits are negative, then you need to do something about this. Why is it that people desire success? There is a desire for growth in each one of us. It is the vast desire for expression and expansion that nature gives to us. This desire manifests in every form of life. If a man change his negative habits, and apply himself to the course of positive actions and opportunities available to him; he will be surprise at the rapid transformation the effect of the change will bring to him; more often than not, in the comfort and material things of life. Thoughts of fear, financial insecurity, doubt, and indecision crystallizes into weak, unmanly, and indecisive habits which solidify into circumstances of failure. On the other hand, a positive and determinate thought of all kinds crystallizes into habits of grace, temperance, courage, self determination and self control. The results of such thought is success, plenty, and freedom of all kind – including financial freedom!

Invest in your Future

Investment opportunities will help you to establish a strong financial base for your future. Think ahead and see how you can put money into viable businesses that can bring good future earnings for you. Do whatever you can to improve your net worth, either by reducing your debt, increasing your savings, or increasing your income, or all of the above. However, this must be with caution because not all investments are good. Observe the business climate of such opportunity before committing yourself. My resolve not to invest in stocks market sometime back cleared me from the trouble that came later. An investment on landed properties for instance, is a good decision. Land appreciates continuously. The growth of your investments over time will be amazing if you start early. Conduct investigation on new business opportunities, but whatever it is, start now. Over the years, if you calculate the worth of your investments, you'll see it grows. And that feels great.

Self-determination is a skill; a skill that you need to constantly use to get better on your performance. Practice it every day. Because the day you stop practicing it is the day you start to lose it. It is a skill that gets better with practice. That means that if you can just begin applying it in one area of your life soon what you learn will transfer to other areas of your life. When you are able to apply self-determination to any area of your life the results will dramatically improve.

On a final note, I'll like you t know that inside of you, there is a little part of you that wants to be completely lazy. Anytime you try to do something worthwhile, that person inside you tries everything possible to get you to stop. The only way to embrace self determination is to have the ability to communicate with this person inside you effectively. I'll warn you though, this person is extremely persuasive. And it's important that you realize this from the beginning. You're not going to win every battle with this person. You simply need to strive to do your best.

About the Author

Victor Peters is a motivational speaker and an ardent practitioner of self-improvement techniques with many years of experience in human capacity building and personal development. He has conducted training to organizations and individuals on personal development and self-improvement. After many years of studying, practicing and gaining practical experience, he decided to share the knowledge and experience he has gained, through his blog, and frequent writings in journals and other book publishing media.

Victor holds a Bachelor of Science (BSc) degree in Computer Science from the University of Wollongong Australia, a Master of Science (MSc) and Doctor of Philosophy (PhD) degree, also in Computer Science from Universiti Malaysia Sarawak (UNIMAS).

Victor Peters is the author of several books, among which are 'Find and Never Lose It', 'Is this Luck or Deliberate Working?', 'Financial Success Tool Kit', Financial Worries? Try This! Power of Thought and Action on your Mind; Financial Wisdom in the Days of Small Beginning; Developing and Spreading your Financial Tentacles; and 'How Best to Tame the Vindictive Monster called Poverty'.